BLOW HIGH, BLOW
(From "CAROUSEL")

tein II
Music by Richard Rodgers

EDELWEISS
(From "THE SOUND OF MUSIC")

Lyrics by Oscar Hammerstein II
Music by Richard Rodgers

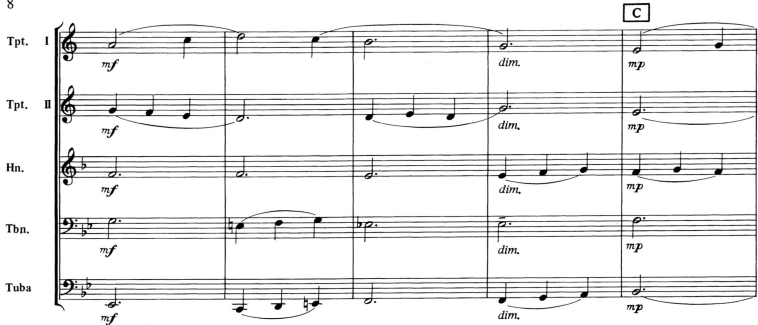

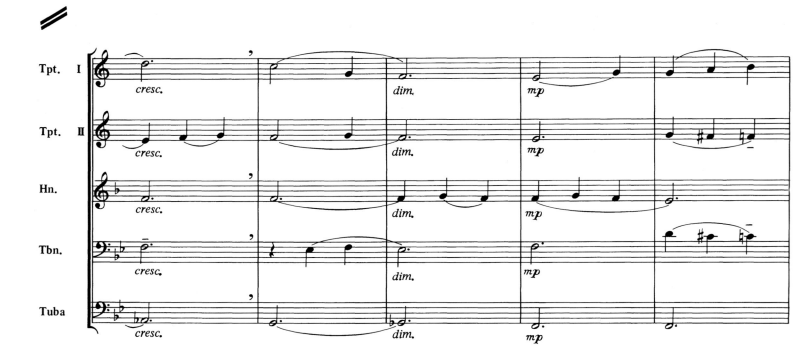

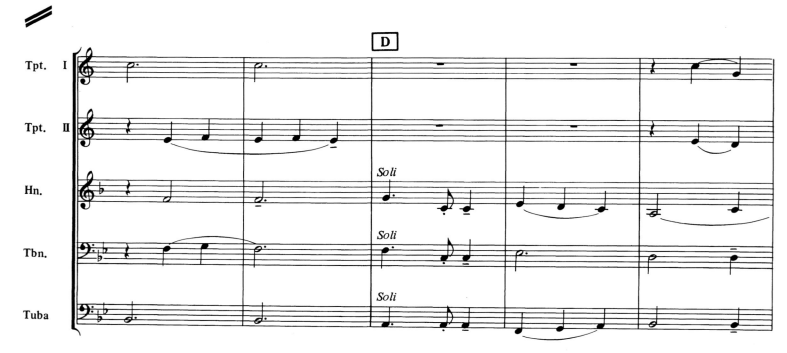

HONEY BUN
From ("South Pacific")

Lyrics by Oscar Hammerstein II
Music by Richard Rodgers

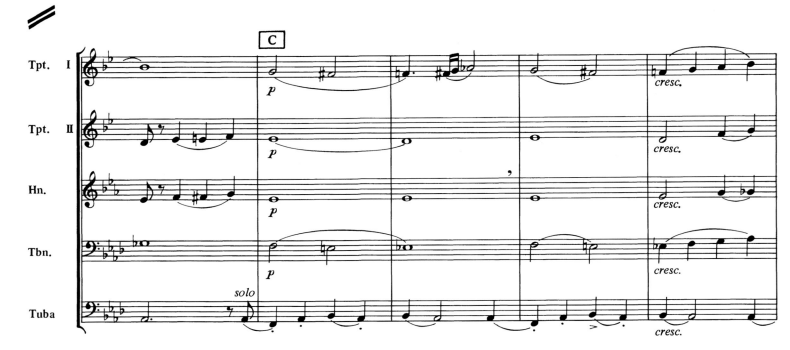

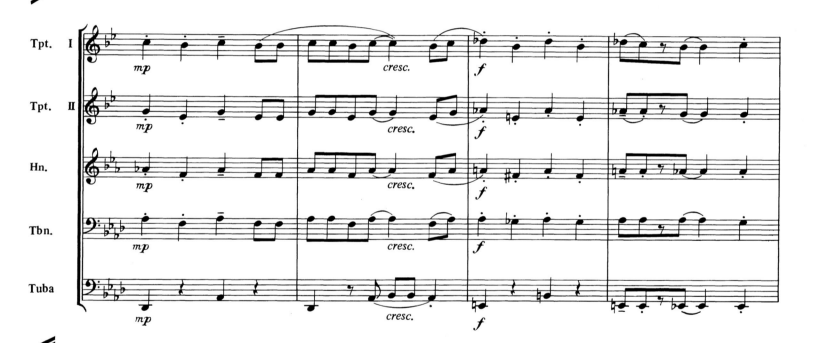

OH, WHAT A BEAUTIFUL MORNIN'
(From "OKLAHOMA!")

Lyrics by Oscar Hammerstein II
Music by Richard Rodgers

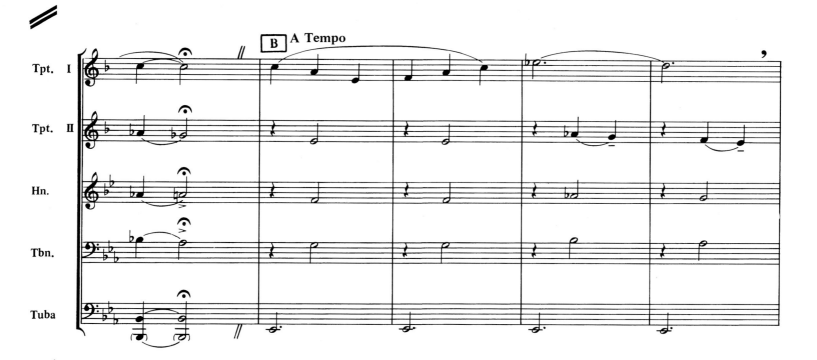

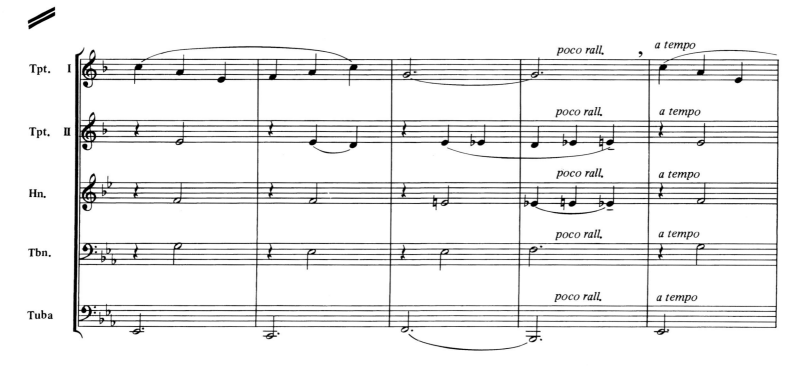

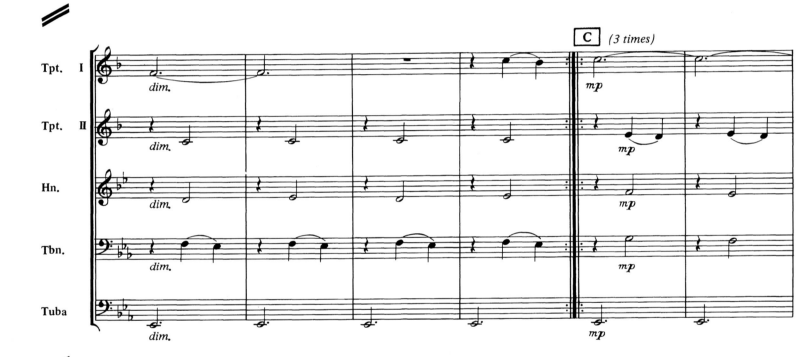

OKLAHOMA
(From "OKLAHOMA!")

Lyrics by Oscar Hammerstein II
Music by Richard Rodgers

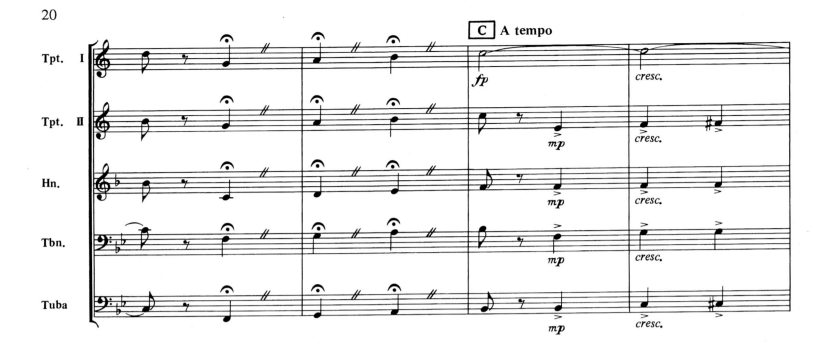

YOU'LL NEVER WALK ALONE
(From "CAROUSEL")

Lyrics by Oscar Hammerstein II
Music by Richard Rodgers

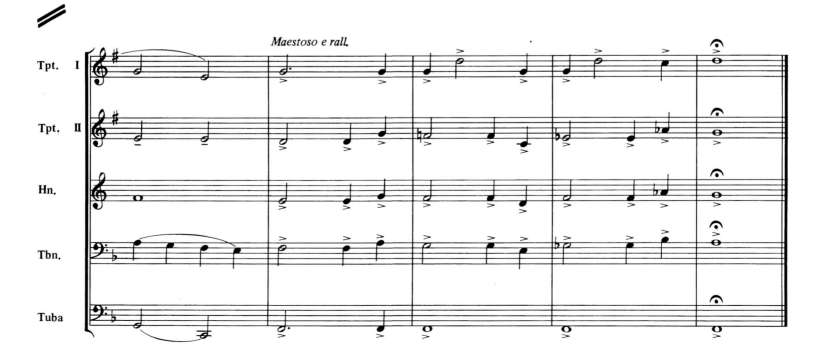